THE DEATH BOOK

PERNILLA STALFELT

A GROUNDWOOD BOOK

death: the act of dying, the end of life.

(from *Webster's Third New International Dictionary*)

Text and pictures copyright © 1999 by Pernilla Stalfelt
Translation copyright © 2002 by Groundwood Books
Translation by Maria Lundin
First published in English by Groundwood Books in 2002
Originally published in Sweden as Döden Boken by
Eriksson & Lindgren in 1999

Groundwood Books / Douglas & McIntyre Ltd.
720 Bathurst Street, Suite 500
Toronto, Ontario M5S 2R4

Distributed in the USA by Publishers Group West
1700 Fourth Street, Berkeley, CA 94710

National Library of Canada Cataloguing in Publication Data
Stalfelt, Pernilla
The death book
Translation of: Döden boken.
ISBN 0-88899-482-6
1. Death—Juvenile literature. I. Title
BF723.D3S75 2002   j306.9.   C2002-900128-5

Library of Congress Control Number: 2002101937

Design: Inger Bodin-Adamsson
Printed and bound in Italy

Sometimes you start thinking about death…

and you might think death is a big mystery.

It's hard to understand what death is…

not only when you're little, but when you're big, too…

It can be hard even if you're really big.

But you can know a little bit anyway.

For example, all plants, animals and humans have to die in the end.

flower   Alfred   flower

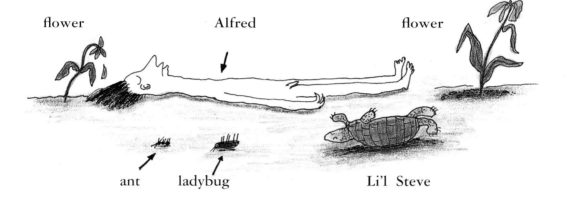

ant   ladybug   Li'l Steve

It's important to make room on the earth for the new ones that are born and starting to grow.

Otherwise the earth would be too full!

wilted flower   seedling

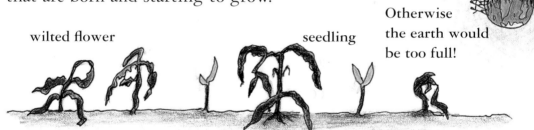

Flowers can get brown and dried out when they die, and lose their petals, whereas people usually get pale and a bit more yellow than normal. They might look as if they're sleeping.

a sleeping person   a dead person

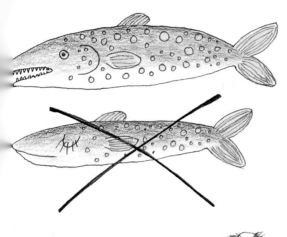

Fish can't close their eyes. They keep them open all the time, even when they're dead.

Most people die when they get too old...

when they don't have the energy to walk around anymore, and when they almost can't cope in a wheelchair either...
when they don't have the energy to laugh or listen or see anymore...
when they are very tired and find everything tiresome and bothersome.
Then they might want to die, so they can finally rest.

Those who are alive, especially kids and baby animals, play and run and laugh and think that it is fun to discover everything

It's not very common for people to die when they are young. But sometimes it does happen. It could be because the person has a serious disease...

or it can happen in an accident, like a car crash.

The ambulance arrives to help out.

Sometimes a baby is already dead when it's born. This could happen to a kitten or to other baby animals as well.

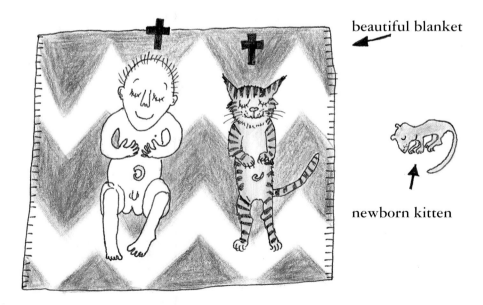

beautiful blanket

newborn kitten

They were only alive inside their moms' bellies, but not outside.

Death can come so fast. One day you have your grandpa.

The next day you may not be able to see him anymore.

Then you feel really empty and sad.

You must be wondering where you go when you die.

Nobody knows for sure,

only those who are already dead.

HELLOO
IS ANYONE
THEERE?

Many people think that when you're dead the soul goes to God.

soul →

body

← They don't notice.

Maybe the soul flies out of the body and is invisible. Then it could fly up to the heavenly kingdom, which might be beyond space somewhere.

God is there, waiting for everyone who has died to arrive...

Maybe God looks like this...

or like this...with a beard.

In the heavenly kingdom, maybe all the dead people turn into angels with wings...

Uncle Angel   Aunt Angel   Elephant Angel

Leopard Angel

Butterfly Angel

Some people don't think that God exists.
They think that it's just black when
you die, and that's it.

Lots of people think black seems pretty boring.
They might hope that it becomes blue instead

or flowery

or gold...

Imagine that you grow out of the earth
as a flower when you die...

or as a tree...

Maybe you turn into
a bird...

Bird and angel
flying together.

Some think you become
a star in the sky.

star with some friends

Maybe you turn into a moose...

The moose flies up to
God for a visit.

What if you become
a hot dog???

NOOOO

You might become a scary
skeleton when you die...

or a regular skeleton that just lies there quietly.

There may be those who turn into vampires...
like Stan, for example.

Once when Stan was going to bite an old lady and
suck her blood…
one thousand mosquitoes came and bit him instead
and sucked his blood!

vampires have
special teeth

Served him right!

Imagine someone turning into a ghost...

who loves scaring people.

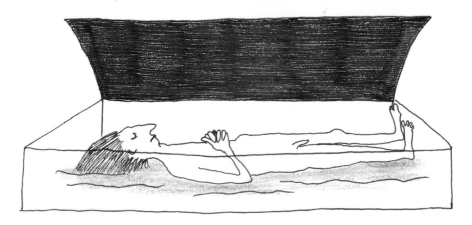

When you die, you might get to lie in a coffin with a lid on.

The coffin goes at the front of a church. People light candles and
decorate with flowers and wreaths to make it look nice.
Sometimes there are flags, too.

Those who knew the dead person may want to send flowers and wreaths, with bows and silk ribbons, to show how much they loved him or her.

When everything is ready in the church, people come and say their last good-byes since they won't see each other again (except in heaven, maybe). It's called a funeral.

The flag is at half-mast.

It used to be that people always wore black clothes at funerals.

Now you can wear whatever you want.

At the funeral there is usually beautiful music and there are
beautiful songs and speeches.

Everyone is very sad.

Some cry a lot...

GRIEF

The crying goes
on inside.

Others are just quiet
and cry inside.

After the funeral everyone usually has coffee together.

When the funeral is over people are often buried in the ground, in the cemetery. Some are buried in their coffins. Then you have to dig a big long hole in the ground.

big hole

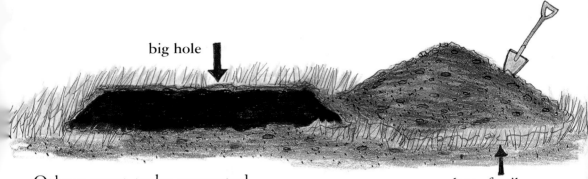

lots of soil

Others want to be cremated.
Then you put the coffin into a big oven. It's so hot inside that the dead person and the coffin are burned up.
What's left are ashes,   which you can put

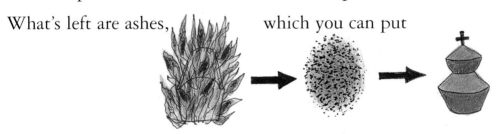

in a beautiful urn=pot.

Then you can bury the urn in the ground. This way you only have to dig a pretty small hole.

a little soil   small hole

When you've covered the coffin or the urn with soil, you can plant flowers on top...or a tree.

Then it becomes a grave. Often you put a gravestone or cross on top of the grave.

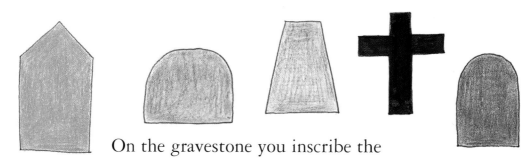

On the gravestone you inscribe the name of the dead person and when he or she was born and died.

The grave is a good place to go to when you want to think about the person who has died. You can read the gravestone, water the flowers and pretend that you're spending time with the person. It's kind of a meeting place.

People can also be buried in a memorial grove.

If you can't visit the grave, you can light a candle instead...and think about the one who is dead.

If you don't have a candle, you can light a sparkler...

You can also remember the dead person by putting on his old hat...

Or you can eat his favorite ice cream and reminisce...

And you can put out a photo of the dead person and build a little altar with beautiful things on it for remembrance.

In the old days you could be buried in a
boat instead of in a coffin.

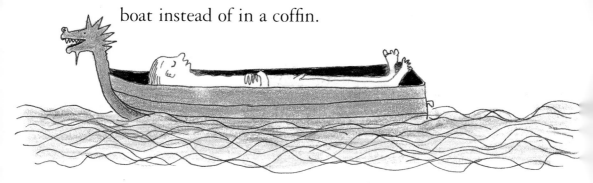

The boat was sent out on the water and burned.
The ocean became the actual grave.

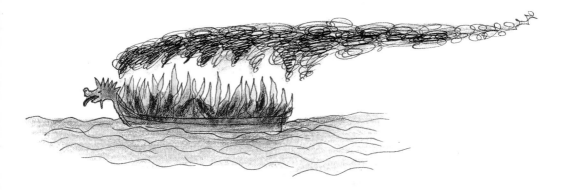

Sometimes people built a grave of stones instead.

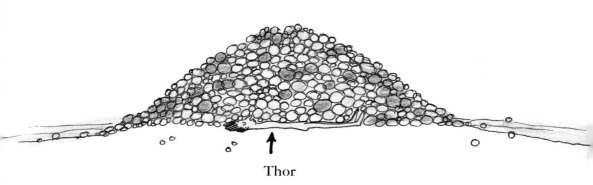

Thor

People used to take their best things with them into the grave, for example:

They could even take their wife or horse and some slaves to help them out in the Kingdom of Death.

That was so they wouldn't be lonely and poor. Important things that they might need went with them to the grave.

Important stuff

Maybe there are mailboxes in the Kingdom of Death?

Nowadays you usually don't take things with you into your grave. Instead you usually write a will. That's done before you die. It's a letter that says who will get your money or things when you are dead.

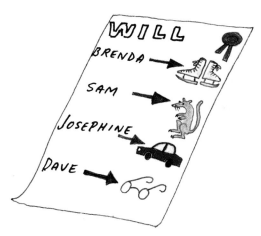

Then there won't have to be any fighting.

Lisa and Paul fighting about Bruno.

Mexicans don't visit graves to be sad...

They go to have a party with a picnic. It's usually on a special day, when they think the dead come back...

to drink coffee, eat their favorite dish and listen to the songs they used to love.

Many of the living dress up like skeletons and cook their favorite foods, make coffee and set off fireworks at the cemetery.

They decorate with skulls made of sugar... or chocolate...

and with lots of flowers and fruit.

When you tell someone about a
person who has died, you can say it
in different ways, for example:
Eva-Maria passed away yesterday.

A long time ago, you could say:
Richard has gone to his Maker.

Sunday best   the coffin

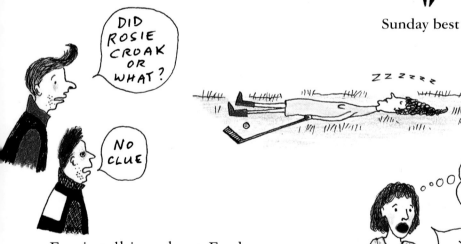

Eva is talking about Fred:

"Did you hear that Dick bit the dust?"

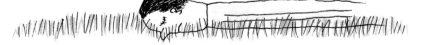

SONG FROM ABOVE

I'm happiest perched on the cloud's gold lining
Near the sun is where I want to be,
There it warms my head, sooths my pining
Soul out in the clear blue, that's me.

Finally I'm free without being lonely
Hovering and floating as only a spirit can,
With Gran and Gramps and Great-Gran, holy
And a little old poodle named Dan.

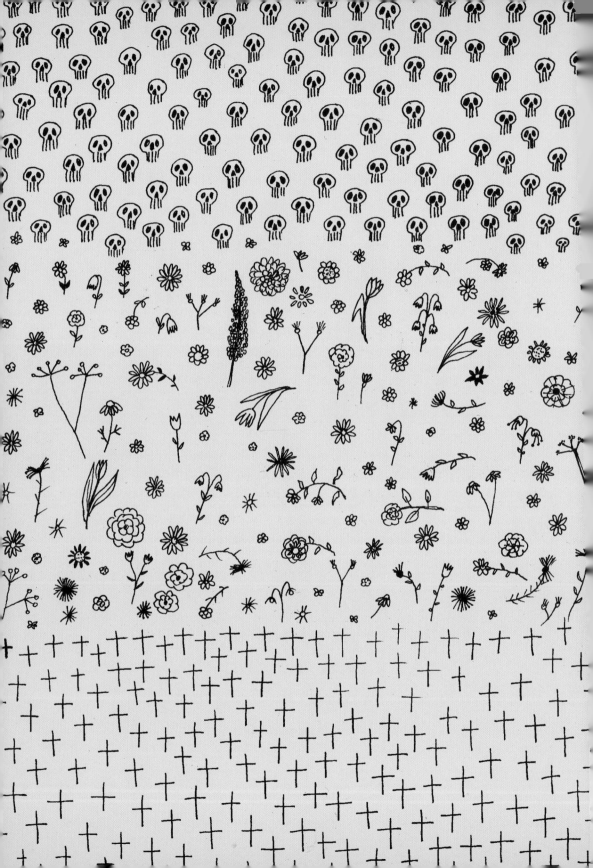